A Blessing
ON THE WAY

A Blessing
ON THE WAY

Counting Each Day While You're Expecting

Sue Christian & Meg Christian

Abingdon Press / Nashville

A Blessing
ON THE WAY
Counting Each Day While You're Expecting

Copyright © 2014 by Abingdon Press

Library of Congress Cataloging-in-Publication Data has been requested.

ISBN 978-1-4267-8060-8

Scripture quotations are from the Common English Bible. Copyright © 2011 by the Common English Bible. All rights reserved. Used by permission. www.CommonEnglishBible.com.

Information about a baby's development is taken from *What to Expect When You're Expecting* by Heidi Murkoff and Sharon Mazel. New York City: Workman Publishing, 2008.

14 15 16 17 18 19 20 21 22 23—10 9 8 7 6 5 4 3 2 1
MANUFACTURED IN THE UNITED STATES OF AMERICA

A mom cannot always leave an inheritance, but every mom can leave a legacy with Jesus Christ. Together, let's take each day of your pregnancy and grow closer to God. In (approximately) 280 days, you will have God's greatest gift in your arms. It is our prayer that each day as you count down to the birth of your baby you will feel God's presence in that day.

Day 280—week 1

Congratulations! You and your husband have created a child in God's image. As your child forms, let's take time to know him or her better.

"God created humanity in God's own image, in the divine image God created them, male and female God created them."

—GENESIS 1:27

Day 279

This is our prayer for you
as you begin this wonderful
adventure of pregnancy.

"May the grace and peace from God
our Father and the Lord Jesus Christ
be with you."

—PHILIPPIANS 1:2

Day 278

*R*ight now God has already
decided the sex of your baby,
but you will have to
wait a while to find out.

"*O*n the day God created humanity,
he made them to resemble God and
created them male and female. He
blessed them and called them humanity
on the day they were created."

—GENESIS 5:1

Day 277

The doctors are going to give
you a lot of information, and
you will read a lot about your
pregnancy. You cannot
do everything they say to do,
so take time to pray
to the Lord for his guidance.

"Listen to instruction, and be wise;
don't avoid it."

—Proverbs 8:33

Day 276

God will be with you every day
of your pregnancy.
Take time to be with him.

"But you, LORD, are my shield! You
are my glory!"

—PSALM 3:3

Day 275

This is a good reminder to take care of your body for yourself and for the new life that is forming inside of you.

"Now be careful not to drink wine or brandy or to eat anything that is ritually unclean, because you are pregnant and will give birth to a son."

—JUDGES 13:4-5

Day 274

You will gain so much wisdom
and instruction from books
in the next months.
Don't forget to include the Bible.

"Wisdom begins with the fear of
the LORD, but fools despise wisdom and
instruction."

—PROVERBS 1:7

Day 273—week 2

When you think of that baby growing inside of you, ponder on what a miracle from God it is!

"Is anything too difficult for the LORD? When I return to you about this time next year, Sarah will have a son."

—GENESIS 18:14

Day 272

On the days when life seems insurmountable, don't rely on your own strength; rely on his.

"So, my child, draw your strength from the grace that is in Christ Jesus."

—2 TIMOTHY 2:1

Day 271

God will be with you
through your
whole pregnancy.
He formed this baby
and will be with you
and this child.

"I'm sure about this: the one who
started a good work in you will stay with
you to complete the job by the day of
Christ Jesus."

—PHILIPPIANS 1:6

Day 270

You may say this to your new
baby as he or she grows up,
but don't forget to apply it
to yourself as you pick up
that same toy ten times!

"Do everything without grumbling
and arguing."

—PHILIPPIANS 2:14

Day 269

It is easy to complain, but don't forget to give thanks to God for all he has given you, starting with this new baby growing inside of you.

"Whatever you do, whether in speech or action, do it all in the name of the Lord Jesus and give thanks to God the Father through him."

—COLOSSIANS 3:17

Day 268

How much more will God's
sacrifice for you mean now that
you are a parent yourself?

"From that time Jesus began to
show his disciples that he had to go
to Jerusalem and suffer many things
from the elders, chief priests, and legal
experts, and that he had to be killed and
raised on the third day."

—MATTHEW 16:21

Day 267

Relax in your pregnancy and realize that God is with you every day and at every step. He keeps his promises—trust in that.

"The LORD set a time and said, 'Tomorrow the LORD will do this in the land.' And the next day the LORD did it."

—EXODUS 9:5

Day 266—week 3

*I*t is your job as a parent to
share God's love with your child.
God told the Israelites to share all
the good he had done for them
with their children. It's not
too early to plan to do the same.

"When in the future your child asks
you, 'What does this mean?' you should
answer, 'The LORD brought us with great
power out of Egypt, out of the place we
were slaves.'" —EXODUS 13:14

CONGRATULATIONS!
YOU HAVE CONCEIVED.
FERTILIZATION HAS
OCCURRED.

Day 265

Take comfort in this statement.
Study your Bible while
you await your new child
and see how it is true.

"The LORD will rule forever
and always."

—EXODUS 15:18

Day 264

You may feel closer to your parents, but do not forget to include your husband's family with this new baby. When you were married, they became your family also.

"Moses listened to his father-in-law's suggestions and did everything that he had said."

—Exodus 18:24

Day 263

Children will be affected by their parents' choices. If you choose a poor path, your child will suffer. But if you choose God's will, you and your family will be blessed.

"I punish children for their parents' sins even to the third and fourth generations of those who hate me. But I am loyal and gracious to the thousandth generation of those who love me and keep my commandments."

—Exodus 20:5-6

Day 262

You are going to be very busy
getting ready for this baby.
Do not forget to set
time apart for God.
This will be especially
important to remember
after your baby is born.

"Remember the Sabbath day
and treat it as holy."

—Exodus 20:8

Day 261

Life is going to change with the
addition of a new family member. It
will be even more important
now than ever to make
your marriage a priority.

"Marriage must be honored
in every respect."

—Hebrews 13:4

Day 260

*I*sn't it amazing that our God
thinks of us as holy people through
the grace of his Son? You may not
feel holy as you gain weight
and get tired, but you are.

"You are holy people to me."

—EXODUS 22:31

Day 259—week 4

God doesn't sleep when you do.
When you and your baby
are sleeping, he will be there
watching you both.

"I lie down, sleep, and wake up
because the LORD helps me."

—PSALM 3:5

EMBRYO HAS REACHED YOUR
UTERUS AND IS IMPLANTING
INTO THE UTERINE LINING.

Day 258

Thank God for that baby
growing inside of you today.

"I will thank you, LORD,
with all my heart."

—PSALM 9:1

Day 257

God thinks so much of you and your baby that he made you in his image and "slightly less than divine."

"What are human beings that you think about them; what are human beings that you pay attention to them? You've made them only slightly less than divine."

—Psalm 8:4-5

Day 256

Jesus can be your "rock" during a
time when everything else in your
life seems to be changing.

"My God is my rock—I take refuge
in him!—he's my shield, my salvation's
strength, my place of safety."

—PSALM 18:2

Day 255

Go and look at the stars tonight.
In the not-too-distant future,
you will be holding your newborn
baby and showing him or her
the stars God made.

"Heaven is declaring God's glory;
the sky is proclaiming his handiwork."

—PSALM 19:1

Day 254

God has been with you right from
the minute you were born
and will be with this new baby
and you as you give birth.

"But you are the one who pulled me
from the womb, placing me safely at my
mother's breasts. I was thrown on you
from birth; you've been my God since I
was in my mother's womb."

—PSALM 22:9-10

EMBRYO IS ABOUT THE SIZE
OF AN ORANGE SEED.

Day 253

_P_ray for your unborn baby.
You will have the greatest
opportunity out of anyone to
share God's love with your child.

"Listen, my son, to your father's
instruction; don't neglect your
mother's teaching."

—PROVERBS 1:8

Day 252—week 5

How will your unborn child
affect the kingdom of God?
How exciting to wait and see!

"Future descendants will serve him;
generations to come will be told about
my Lord. They will proclaim God's
righteousness to those not yet born,
telling them what God has done."

—Psalm 22:30-31

Day 251

Each morning as you lie in bed after you have woken up, lift up your prayers to God. Think of how excited you will be to hear your baby's voice in the morning. God is just as excited to hear yours.

"Lord, in the morning you hear my voice. In the morning I lay it all out before you. Then I wait expectantly."

—Psalm 5:3

Day 250

They say a pregnant woman's face glows with her pregnancy. Special things from God make us all glow.

"Moses came down from Mount Sinai. As he came down from the mountain with the two covenant tablets in his hand, Moses didn't realize that the skin of his face shone brightly because he had been talking with God."

—Exodus 34:29

Day 249

*W*hat wonderful words to remember as you begin the journey of parenthood. Deal with the sins of your child and then remember them no more.

"But don't remember the sins of my youth or my wrongdoing. Remember me only according to your faithful love for the sake of your goodness, Lord."

—PSALM 25:7

HEART BEGINS TO DEVELOP.

Day 248

Praying and raising your child in a godly fashion will help your child have the best start you can give him or her. Your children will be parents some day, so you are helping the next generation.

"They will live a good life, and their descendants will possess the land."

—Psalm 25:13

Day 247

As you are beginning your pregnancy, there will always be things that will make you anxious. Go to God with your fears and know he is always with you.

"The Lord is my light and my salvation. Should I fear anyone? The Lord is a fortress protecting my life. Should I be frightened of anything?"

—Psalm 27:1

MEASURED FROM CROWN TO RUMP, EMBRYO IS ABOUT THE SIZE OF A NAIL HEAD.

Day 246

If you feel you have nothing else to be thankful for today, simply thank God for his love.

"Give thanks to the God of heaven—God's faithful love lasts forever."

—PSALM 136:26

Day 245—week 6

Even King David realized God was his strength. You have been blessed with this pregnancy, but you are also filling many other roles—wife, worker, friend, daughter, and so on. Lean on him at all times, and don't forget to praise him too!

"The LORD is my strength and my shield. My heart trusts him. I was helped, my heart rejoiced, and I thank him with my song."

—PSALM 28:7

Day 244

$\mathcal{L}$ ife will give us some difficulties.
You are setting out on a journey
with a new life. Take time to learn
about God so you can trust him with
your and your baby's future.

"But me? I trust you, LORD!
I affirm, 'You are my God.' My
future is in your hands."

—PSALM 31:14-15

Day 243

We are all sinners and fall short
of the glory of God.
Before you bring this
new life into the world,
resolve any sins
that are still in your life.

"'I'll confess my sins to the LORD,' is
what I said. Then you removed the guilt
of my sin."

—PSALM 32:5

Day 242

Let this bring you comfort as you
go through these nine months and
the years of child-rearing.
God is always with you.

"The Lord looks down from
heaven; he sees every human being."

—Psalm 33:13

Day 241

Let's think about every woman
reading this book lifting up
God today! Can't you see
God smiling at this?

"Magnify the LORD with me!
Together let us lift his name up high!"

—PSALM 34:3

Day 240

Your baby has refuge inside
of you. You can lean on God
and take refuge in him.

"The one who takes refuge in him
is truly happy!"

—PSALM 34:8

Day 239

Don't let your baby become your god. Your baby will need you, but you still must find time for your husband and for God.

"You must not bow down to another god, because the LORD is passionate: the LORD's name means 'a passionate God.'"

—EXODUS 34:14

YOUR BABY HAS A HEARTBEAT.

Day 238—week 7

In raising your baby to know God,
you also will be giving yourself
a gift because the Bible teaches
children that they should respect
you and your husband.

"Each of you must respect your
mother and father, and you must keep
my sabbaths; I am the LORD your God."

—LEVITICUS 19:3

Day 237

$\mathcal{H}$aving a baby can overwhelm
you. Be sure to keep your priorities
correct and get up earlier
so you can get to church.

"You must keep my sabbaths and
respect my sanctuary; I am the LORD."

—LEVITICUS 26:2

MOUTH AND TONGUE ARE
FORMING. SO ARE ARM
AND LEG BUDS.

Day 236

This was Moses speaking to God about the Israelites. Even Moses could not handle all that was going on in his life, so he went straight to God. There will be things you cannot handle in your pregnancy, so follow Moses's example and go straight to God.

"I can't bear this people on my own. They're too heavy for me."

—Numbers 11:14

Kidneys are in place.

Day 235

Take time in your pregnancy to rest and seek God. It will help you keep your priorities right.

"You will seek the LORD your God from there, and you will find him if you seek him with all your heart and with all your being."

—DEUTERONOMY 4:29

Day 234

*Y*ou cannot recite the words of the Lord to your baby if you do not take time now to learn them.

"Love the LORD your God with all your heart, all your being, and all your strength. These words that I am commanding you today must always be on your minds. Recite them to your children."

—DEUTERONOMY 6:5-7

Day 233

Isn't it amazing that what you
teach your newborn baby
could be taught to
the thousandth generation?

"He is the faithful God, who
keeps the covenant and proves loyal to
everyone who loves him and keeps his
commands—even to the thousandth
generation!"

—Deuteronomy 7:9

BABY IS THE SIZE OF A
LARGE RASPBERRY.

Day 232

God loves you like a father, as you will love your new little one, and because we love our children, we must discipline them in love.

"Know then in your heart that the LORD your God has been disciplining you just as a father disciplines his children."

—DEUTERONOMY 8:5

HEART RATE IS 150 BEATS PER MINUTE.

Day 231—week 8

The Bible speaks often of how God protects us in "the shadow of his wings." On the days that your pregnancy seems too difficult, think of this.

"Humanity finds refuge in the shadow of your wings."

—Psalm 36:7

YOUR BABY CAN MAKE SPONTANEOUS MOVEMENTS.

Day 230

Concentrate your energies
on this new being you are
bringing forth and pray
for people who disappoint you.

"Don't get upset over evildoers;
don't be jealous of those who do wrong,
because they will fade fast, like grass."

—PSALM 37:1

Day 229

With your hormones raging, you
may have to try even harder than
normal to let go of anger
and the things that hurt you!

"Let go of anger and leave rage
behind! Don't get upset—it will only
lead to evil."

—Psalm 37:8

Day 228

For all of the moms who may feel as if they are facing this pregnancy alone, know that you are never alone! God will always be there.

"I have never seen the righteous left all alone.... They are always gracious and generous. Their children are a blessing."

—Psalm 37:25-26

Day 227

$\mathscr{I}$n all the excitement of
the new baby, don't forget
how great your God is.

"The LORD is great and
so worthy of praise!"

—PSALM 48:1

Day 226

*R*emember even in difficult times
that he is always there for you!

"God is our refuge and strength,
a help always near in times of great
trouble."

—Psalm 46:1

Now your embryo
is a fetus.

Day 225

*Y*ou will sing to your baby often. Sing with joy, sing to your unborn baby, and sing to God!

"Sing praises to God! Sing praises!"

—Psalm 47:6

YOUR BABY IS ABOUT ONE INCH IN LENGTH.

Day 224—week 9

Take time today at stop lights,
at the fridge, in the bathroom
(in pregnancy this could be often!),
and while changing channels
to praise God!

"The Lord is great and so worthy
of praise!"

—Psalm 48:1

TINY MUSCLES ARE
STARTING TO FORM.

Day 223

$\mathscr{D}$uring your day, look for God's blessings and listen for his voice. Life with a newborn will be busy, but God will still be speaking to you if you take the time to listen.

"From the rising of the sun to where it sets, God, the LORD God, speaks."

—PSALM 50:1

YOU MAY BE ABLE TO HEAR THE HEARTBEAT AT YOUR DOCTOR'S OFFICE.

Day 222

This verse is telling a parent to
teach your child about God.
There are a lot of false philosophies
in the world, so look
to the Bible and not man.

"Teach them to your children, by
talking about them when you are sitting
around your house and when you are out
and about, when you are lying down and
when you are getting up."

—DEUTERONOMY 11:19

Day 221

As a mom, you may worry that your children will think you are playing favorites with one or another. It can be hard for the firstborn to adjust to a new baby, but it will come. Isn't it wonderful we have a God who loves us each the same?

"The LORD your God is the God of all gods and Lord of all lords, the great, mighty, and awesome God who doesn't play favorites."

—DEUTERONOMY 10:17

Day 220

God is so good
to forgive us.
Take this
as a model
as you parent
this new baby.

"Wipe away my wrongdoings
according to your great compassion!"

—PSALM 51:1

Day 219

God is a God of joy. Wake up
in the morning thinking of all the
wonderful things he has done
for you—starting with
that new baby inside of you!

"I will sing of your strength! In the
morning I will shout out loud about
your faithful love because you have been
my stronghold, my shelter when I was
distraught."

—PSALM 59:16

Day 218

During these nine months, there
will be many wonderful things but
also some difficult things.
Turn to God and his word
to help you through.

"Only God is my rock and my
salvation—my stronghold!—I will
not be shaken."

—Psalm 62:6

BONES AND CARTILAGE
ARE FORMING.

Day 217—week 10

God hears you. Nothing is too small
to bring before God, whether it is
morning sickness, tiredness,
or simply praise for this new life.

"But God definitely listened.
He heard the sound of my prayer."

—Psalm 66:19

 Your baby's elbows
are working.

Day 216

It is hard to think of
your unborn baby having children,
but in time, you will most likely have
grandchildren. What a comfort
to know God will
be there for them too!

"I will set up my covenant with you
and your descendants after you in every
generation as an enduring covenant. I
will be your God and your descendants'
God after you."

—GENESIS 17:7

Day 215

You can't know everything about
parenting, so trust that
God will provide you with what
you need to know and
don't be afraid to ask for help.

"Trust in the LORD with all
your heart; don't rely on your own
intelligence. Know him in all your paths,
and he will keep your ways straight."

—PROVERBS 3:5-6

Day 214

When it is time to correct your little one, realize you are doing so because you love him or her and don't want the behavior to continue. To give in to everything is easy, but it is not the best for a child.

"The LORD loves those he corrects, just like a father who treats his son with favor."

—PROVERBS 3:12

TEETH ARE FORMING UNDER THE GUMS.

Day 213

*Y*ou will guard what your baby
sees and hears. You must also be
careful what you see and hear.
It is amazing what little ones pick up.

"More than anything you guard,
protect your mind, for life flows from it."

—Proverbs 4:23

Day 212

Take time to learn about your baby so you can be prepared and not caught off guard.
That is part of the reason God gave you these nine months.

"Wisdom is better than pearls."

—PROVERBS 8:11

YOUR BABY IS ABOUT
2 INCHES LONG.

Day 211

$\mathcal{N}$ot only did God create your baby but he also created you. You are a very special person to God. Take time to feel that.

"The LORD created me."

—PROVERBS 8:22

FINGERNAILS AND TOENAILS
ARE BEGINNING TO FORM.

Day 210—week 11

You need to be careful about
your nutrition because you are
eating for two, and you
also need to be careful
what you are feeding your soul.

"Jesus replied, 'It's written, People
won't live only by bread, but by every
word spoken by God.'"

—MATTHEW 4:4

Day 209

You will be all-consumed with your baby at first, but don't forget who you are and all the talents God gave you. Make time for them. You are important too!

"In the same way, let your light shine before people, so they can see the good things you do and praise your Father who is in heaven."

—MATTHEW 5:16

Day 208

Nothing is more
important in life
than your relationship
with Jesus.

"And now, little children, remain
in relationship to Jesus, so that when he
appears we can have confidence and not
be ashamed in front of him when
he comes."

—1 JOHN 2:28

Day 207

Mothers are amazing people. Some at-home mothers think they are not doing as much for the world as those who work, but nothing could be further from the truth! Working moms and at-home moms take note: it is your heart that pleases God and brings you honor.

"A gracious woman gains honor."

—PROVERBS 11:16

Day 206

$\mathcal{A}$t this time, you are putting a
lot of thought into your new baby,
which is natural. Don't forget
though to think of others.

"Generous persons will prosper;
those who refresh others will themselves
be refreshed."

—Proverbs 11:25

Day 205

It will be important to model and teach your new child about helping others. Is there some way of putting this into practice in your life now?

"Whenever you give to the poor, don't blow your trumpet as the hypocrites do in the synagogues and in the streets so that they may get praise from people."

—MATTHEW 6:2

YOUR BABY IS ABOUT 2 1/2 INCHES AND 1/2 OUNCE.

Day 204

It is amazing, once you find out you're pregnant, how unimportant the things you used to value may seem. Your belongings are no longer as important as this new little child of God.

"Stop collecting treasures for your own benefit…and where thieves break in and steal them. Instead, collect treasures for yourselves in heaven…. Where your treasure is, there your heart will be also."

—MATTHEW 6:19, 21

Day 203—week 12

Isn't it wonderful to know you
have a God who will always
be with you no matter what
you are going through?

"Be my rock of refuge where
I can always escape."

—Psalm 71:3

The digestive system
is practicing
contraction
movements.

Day 202

God created your new baby and
will know the time to allow
your child to be born
and released from your womb.

"You, LORD, are the one I've trusted
since childhood. I've depended on you
from birth—you cut the cord when
I came from my mother's womb."

—PSALM 71:5-6

BONE MARROW IS MAKING
WHITE BLOOD CELLS.

Day 201

It is good to be reminded
of all that God has done for you
and dwell on everything
God did in history.

"I will dwell on your mighty acts,
my Lord."

—PSALM 71:16

Day 200

A righteous person can rest easy at night, as they have done what is pleasing to God. Make an effort—especially now that you are a parent—to live in an upright manner.

"Let the righteous flourish throughout their lives, and let peace prosper until the moon is no more."

—Psalm 72:7

Day 199

As your body changes, take this
verse to heart and realize
that this is a period of life
and what is important
is who you are on the inside.

"Therefore, I say to you, don't worry
about your life, what you'll eat or what
you'll drink, or about your body, what
you'll wear. Isn't life more than food and
the body more than clothes?"

—MATTHEW 6:25

Day 198

*M*ay we all desire and strive
to desire only God.

"There's nothing on earth I desire
except you."

—Psalm 73:25

Your baby is about
3 inches long.

Day 197

The Bible is so clear and simple
yet at times so hard to follow.
This is a verse for everyone to work
on each day.

"Don't judge, so that
you won't be judged."

—MATTHEW 7:1

YOUR BABY'S VOCAL CORDS
ARE DEVELOPING.

Day 196—week 13

As you bring up your new baby, remember not to keep him or her isolated with only Christians. We are supposed to be the light for the world. The Bible says that we are not supposed to be OF the world, but it does say to be IN it.

"As Jesus sat down to eat in Matthew's house, many tax collectors and sinners joined Jesus and his disciples at the table."

—Matthew 9:10

Day 195

Begin praying that your child
will hear the will of God
in his or her life and obey it.

"Then he said to his disciples, 'The
size of the harvest is bigger than you can
imagine, but there are few workers.'"

—MATTHEW 9:37

Day 194

Rest in the fact that the God
who created the universe created
you and your new baby.
He knows the number of
hairs on your head and already
that of your baby in your womb.

"Even the hairs of your head are all
counted. Don't be afraid. You are worth
more than many sparrows."

—MATTHEW 10:30-31

Day 193

A pregnant woman is carrying
a lot on her plate. Take some
quiet time with God to rest—
add a cup of herbal tea!

"Come to me, all you who are
struggling hard and carrying heavy loads,
and I will give you rest."

—MATTHEW 11:28

Day 192

Don't forget that
Jesus needed time alone.
If he needed time to pray,
how much more
do we need it!

"When he sent them away, he went
up onto a mountain by himself to pray."

—MATTHEW 14:23

Day 191

$\mathscr{C}$hildren have such trust;
we can learn from them.

"Then he called a little child over
to sit among the disciples, and said, 'I
assure you that if you don't turn your
lives around and become like this little
child, you will definitely not enter the
kingdom of heaven.'"

—MATTHEW 18:2-3

Day 190

You have created this child;
imagine how much you will love him
or her! Now imagine the God who
created you—he loves you even
more than you love your child!

"Isn't he your father, your creator?
Didn't he make you and establish you?"

—Deuteronomy 32:6

Day 189—week 14

$\mathcal{T}$ake comfort in the fact that
God knows all your hardships
and will hold people accountable.
You do not have to.

"The wicked are destroyed and are
no more, but the family of the righteous
will endure."

—Proverbs 12:7

Beginning of
Second Trimester

Day 188

God isn't talking just about money here but about memories, being role models, times together, teaching children about God, and so on. The money your child has may be out of your control. You choose what memories and teachings he or she is left with.

"Good people leave their grandchildren an inheritance."

—PROVERBS 13:22

YOUR BABY COULD SPROUT HAIR NOW.

Day 187

*A*t times as a new mom, you may
want to seek out other Christian
moms to pray and help guide you.

"*A*ll were united in their devotion
to prayer, along with some women,
including Mary the mother of Jesus, and
his brothers."

—ACTS 1:14

YOUR BABY IS STARTING
TO GROW EYEBROWS.

Day 186

Paul loved Jesus with a passion.
As Christian moms, we need
to study the word to gain
the same passion about our Lord.

"Unhindered and with complete
confidence, [Paul] continued to preach
God's kingdom and to teach about the
Lord Jesus Christ."

—ACTS 28:31

Day 185

Don't compare yourself
to anyone else.
God loves you
just the way you are.

"God does not have favorites."

—ROMANS 2:11

Day 184

Even if you are going through a
rough time right now, rest in the
fact that God knows the whole
picture and will work
all things out for his good.

"We know that God works all
things together for good for the ones
who love God, for those who are called
according to his purpose."

—ROMANS 8:28

YOUR BABY IS ABOUT
4 1/2 INCHES.

Day 183

A verse to memorize
and share.

"Because if you confess with your
mouth 'Jesus is Lord' and in your heart
you have faith that God raised him from
the dead, you will be saved."

—ROMANS 10:9

YOUR BABY CAN WIGGLE ITS
FINGERS, SUCK ITS THUMB,
BREATHE, AND SWALLOW.

Day 182—week 15

You will see a lot of baby "stuff" that advertisements will tell you that you need. This baby will only need parents who love him or her and a God who loves him or her even more! The world has different values than God does.

"Don't be conformed to the patterns of this world, but be transformed by the renewing of your minds so that you can figure out what God's will is—what is good and pleasing and mature."

—ROMANS 12:2

Day 181

How exciting to think about your baby and all the possibilities for him or her. Your baby may have totally different gifts to use than you.

"We have different gifts that are consistent with God's grace that has been given to us."

—ROMANS 12:6

Day 180

Just as you love the baby you helped create, try to love each person as God's creation.

"Love each other like the members of your family. Be the best at showing honor to each other."

—ROMANS 12:10

Day 179

If you do a Lamaze class or go to
a mom's group, find that lady who
might be a bit shy and welcome her.

"So welcome each other, in the
same way that Christ also welcomed you,
for God's glory."

—ROMANS 15:7

Day 178

Does someone come to mind
for whom you can pray this prayer
(your husband, other children,
friend, sibling, and so on)?

"May the God of hope fill you with
all joy and peace in faith so that you
overflow with hope by the power of the
Holy Spirit."

—ROMANS 15:13

Day 177

God didn't wait until we had it all together to save us. Love (not condone) even the side of your new child that may try your patience.

"God shows his love for us, because while we were still sinners Christ died for us."

—Romans 5:8

Your baby is about 4 ounces.

Day 176

Do not be too hard on yourself
if you don't know everything about
your new baby or make mistakes.
Everyone makes mistakes, and that is
why God's grace is so amazing.

"All have sinned and fall short
of God's glory."

—ROMANS 3:23

Day 175—week 16

This is a verse to keep
in our minds as we
go about our day.

"Therefore, you should treat people
in the same way that you want people
to treat you; this is the Law and the
Prophets."

—MATTHEW 7:12

BABY'S EYES ARE WORKING.

Day 174

Who comes to your mind when you read this? Write a card to him or her today and tell him or her.

"I thank my God always for you, because of God's grace that was given to you in Christ Jesus."

—1 CORINTHIANS 1:4

Day 173

God is preparing this new baby
inside just for you and your family.
No other child will be like yours.
He or she will be made
especially for you by God.

"God has prepared things for those
who love him that no eye has seen, or
ear has heard, or that haven't crossed the
mind of any human being."

—1 CORINTHIANS 2:9

Day 172

Babies have stages to go through
to reach adulthood. In your journey
with God, you will have different
seasons of learning.
Be patient with yourself
as you will be with your baby.

"I gave you milk to drink instead of
solid food, because you weren't up to it
yet."

—1 Corinthians 3:2

Day 171

*J*ust as you are trying to eat
right for the baby growing in you,
try to fill your mind
with thoughts that are godly.

"Don't you know that you are God's
temple and God's Spirit lives in you?"

—1 CORINTHIANS 3:16

Day 170

It is so easy to make a promise
but harder to keep it.

"Make promises to the LORD your
God and keep them!"

—PSALM 76:11

YOUR BABY IS PALM-SIZE NOW,
ABOUT 5 INCHES AND 5 OUNCES.

Day 169

The Bible is really a book to study
and learn from. No matter how many
times you read it, you continue
to learn so much. You will be busy
at each stage of your baby's life,
so start right now
and make the Bible a priority.

"I will meditate on all your works."

—PSALM 77:12

Day 168—week 17

People will give you a lot of
advice with this new baby.
Listen, and the Holy Spirit
will help you discern what is right.

"Fools see their own way as right,
but the wise listen to advice."

—PROVERBS 12:15

Day 167

Your new baby will teach you so much as he or she grows. A child's innocence, faith, and trust are things we start to lose as we get older.

"At that time the disciples came to Jesus and asked, 'Who is the greatest in the kingdom of heaven?' Then he called a little child over to sit among the disciples, and said, 'I assure you that if you don't turn your lives around and become like this little child, you will definitely not enter the kingdom of heaven.'"

—MATTHEW 18:1-3

Day 166

God is knitting your baby together, today and every day of your pregnancy.

"You are the one who created my innermost parts; you knit me together while I was still in my mother's womb."

—PSALM 139:13

Day 165

It is important not to be overly self-centered, and it's especially easy to do this when you're pregnant. Look for ways to lift your husband and family up.

"All who lift themselves up will be brought low. But all who make themselves low will be lifted up."

—MATTHEW 23:12

Day 164

Even Jesus did not want to suffer
what he knew was coming. We can
learn so much from his desire to do
God's will. During your delivery,
know Jesus can relate
to your body being in pain.

"My Father, if it's possible, take
this cup of suffering away from me.
However—not what I want but what
you want."

—MATTHEW 26:39

Day 163

Even though sometimes
your road may be difficult,
Jesus will always be with you.

"Look, I myself will be with you
every day until the end of this
present age."

—MATTHEW 28:20

Day 162

Every mother thinks her baby is special, and she should! But be careful in bragging to other people—you can share your joys of parenthood and baby's achievements without being arrogant. It's okay to admit you don't have it all together as a parent.

"Knowledge makes people arrogant, but love builds people up. If anyone thinks they know something, they don't yet know as much as they should know. But if someone loves God, then they are known by God."

—1 CORINTHIANS 8:1-3

Day 161—week 18

*K*eeping your eyes
on God is the best
way to not be tempted.

"But God is faithful. He won't allow
you to be tempted beyond your abilities.
Instead, with the temptation, God will
also supply a way out so that you will be
able to endure it."

—1 CORINTHIANS 10:13

YOUR BABY CAN HICCUP.

Day 160

You will be blessed by different people coming into your life to support your new family. God gives each person different gifts, and these different people will help you in your parenting journey.

"Christ is just like the human body—a body is a unit and has many parts; and all the parts of the body are one body, even though there are many."

—1 CORINTHIANS 12:12

Day 159

Your children will be taught by what they see you doing. If you put God first, you are teaching them what is important in your life.

"…ordering our ancestors to teach them to their children. This is so that the next generation and children not yet born will know these things, and so they can rise up and tell their children to put their hope in God."

—Psalm 78:5-7

Your baby has its own unique fingerprints and toe prints.

Day 158

God took care
of the Israelites
when they left Egypt.
You can trust in him
to take care of you
during your pregnancy.

"God sent provisions
to satisfy them."

—Psalm 78:25

Day 157

Try to look at the positive
side to each situation
you come upon today.
It will surely light up your face.

"A joyful heart brightens one's face,
but a troubled heart breaks the spirit."

—PROVERBS 15:13

Day 156

*W*hatever you do today, even the smallest task, try to do it for the Lord. This can make even the most menial task feel important.

"Commit your work to the LORD, and your plans will succeed. The LORD made everything for a purpose."

—PROVERBS 16:3-4

YOUR BABY IS ABOUT 6 INCHES LONG AND 1/2 POUND.

Day 155

Your pregnancy may have been a surprise, but nothing surprises God. Each day the Lord knows what you will face and be with you at every step.

"People plan their path, but the LORD secures their steps."

—PROVERBS 16:9

Day 154—week 19

God picked you to be the mother
of this newborn baby.
It was not a mistake but a gift
to this child and you.

"Grandchildren are the crown
of the elderly, and the glory of children
is their parents."

—PROVERBS 17:6

Day 153

Your child will take your family
name and, with that, who your family
has become. If there are
some things you need to fix,
now is the time to do so.

"The righteous live with integrity;
happy are their children who come
after them."

—PROVERBS 20:7

Day 152

$\mathscr{D}$uring the especially hard days during your pregnancy, remember that this is all for a great reward— your child. This should help make any difficulty associated with your pregnancy a little bit better.

"So don't throw away your confidence—it brings a great reward. You need to endure so that you can receive the promises after you do God's will."

—HEBREWS 10:35-36

Day 151

*Y*our choices greatly affect
this new baby, so choose
a life lived for God!

"Now choose life—so that you and
your descendants will live—by loving the
LORD your God, by obeying his voice,
and by clinging to him."

—DEUTERONOMY 30:19-20

Day 150

If you have any questions
about Jesus, please call a pastor
of a Bible-believing church
to help you answer any questions.
It is a pastor's greatest joy
to help someone know Jesus.

"God so loved the world that he
gave his only Son, so that everyone who
believes in him won't perish but will
have eternal life."

—JOHN 3:16

Day 149

*I*t is amazing how many times in the Bible God directs us to instruct our children in his ways. You have a clean slate with this new baby!

"You must return to the LORD your God, obeying his voice, in line with all that I'm commanding you right now— you and your children—with all your mind and with all your being."

—DEUTERONOMY 30:2

YOUR BABY IS ABOUT 6 1/2 INCHES AND 10 OUNCES.

Day 148

It is a blessing to teach your children about Jesus. You will find that you will learn along with them as they ask you questions that you might not know the answers to.

"In the future your children may ask, 'What do these stones mean to you?' Then you will tell them that the water of the Jordan was cut off before the LORD's covenant chest."

—JOSHUA 4:6-7

Day 147—week 20

What a comfort to realize that
the God who created you
will always be there
for your newborn baby!

"We will give you thanks forever;
we will proclaim your praises from one
generation to the next."

—PSALM 79:13

IF YOUR BABY IS A GIRL, HER
UTERUS IS FULLY DEVELOPED,
AND IF A BOY, HIS TESTICLES
HAVE BEGUN THEIR DESCENT
FROM THE ABDOMEN.

Day 146

The closer you grow to God,
the more you can trust him
in difficult times.

"Those who trust in you are
truly happy."

—PSALM 84:12

Day 145

Even right this second,
God is forming your baby.
What a miracle it is!

"Ears to hear and eyes to see—
the LORD made them both."

—PROVERBS 20:12

Day 144

You and your husband
will become your baby's most
important role models in life.

"The righteous live with integrity;
happy are their children who come
after them."

—PROVERBS 20:7

Day 143

God will be present
with your new baby
from birth
until old age.

"[You] who have been borne by
me since pregnancy, whom I carried
from the womb until you grow old. I am
the one, and until you turn gray I will
support you."

—Isaiah 46:3-4

Day 142

$\mathcal{O}$nce something comes out of
your mouth, you can't take it back.
At this point in your life, you are
most likely tired of being pregnant,
so take some time before you speak.
Most people who insult us
don't even realize
they've said something wrong—
most people aren't out to get us!

"Those who guard their mouths
and their tongues guard themselves
from trouble."

—PROVERBS 21:23

Day 141

When your child is old enough
to make the decision that
Christ is his or her Lord,
take him or her somewhere
to be baptized and say it publicly.

"John was in the wilderness calling
for people to be baptized to show that
they were changing their hearts and lives
and wanted God to forgive their sins."

—MARK 1:4

YOUR BABY IS ABOUT
7 INCHES AND 11 OUNCES.

Day 140—week 21

You are related
to God in a personal way.
Rejoice in that.

"Whoever does God's will is my
brother, sister, and mother."

—MARK 3:35

BABY'S CARTILAGE
IS TURNING INTO BONE.

Day 139

Everyone's faith
can grow stronger.
This prayer is an honest
and earnest
prayer to God.

"I have faith; help my lack of faith!"

—MARK 9:24

Day 138

This passage tells us so much. We need to have faith like little children, and you're about to learn exactly what that means! Watch how much you will learn from your new baby (how to stop and enjoy the moment, to truly enjoy food and not just shovel it in, and so on).

"'I assure you that whoever doesn't welcome God's kingdom like a child will never enter it.' Then he hugged the children and blessed them."

—MARK 10:15-16

Day 137

Reading the Old Testament gives
one hope in the promises of God.
He is always with you at every stage
of your pregnancy. Rest in that.

"Not one of all the good things
that the LORD had promised to the
house of Israel failed. Every promise
was fulfilled."

—JOSHUA 21:45

Day 136

There are going to be so many
new distractions as you raise
this new baby, but never
leave God out of your day.

"Hold on to him and serve him with
all your heart and being."

—JOSHUA 22:5

Day 135

*Y*ou and your husband
will set the standard for
how your child will live. Will you
choose to live for God or not?

"But my family and I will serve
the LORD."

—JOSHUA 24:15

Day 134

God knew of his plans for your
child before you even conceived
him or her. When you start
to worry about your child's future,
remember God already has
a perfect plan for him or her.

"Before I created you in the womb
I knew you; before you were born I set
you apart."

—JEREMIAH 1:5

Day 133—week 22

Instead of turning on the news
today, take some time to read God's
word. The news brings stress
over events we can't control.
The Bible gives us peace
knowing God does have control.

"LORD of heavenly forces, those who
trust in you are truly happy!"

—PSALM 84:12

YOUR BABY COULD LIVE
OUTSIDE OF YOU AS OF TODAY.

Day 132

God always hears you
when you cry out to him.

"Know this: the LORD takes personal
care of the faithful. The LORD will hear
me when I cry out to him."

—PSALM 4:3

YOUR BABY CAN HEAR THE
SOUND OF YOUR VOICE.

Day 131

Make this your prayer
for today and for
the rest of your life.

"Teach me your way, LORD, so that
I can walk in your truth. Make my heart
focused only on honoring your name."

—PSALM 86:11

YOUR BABY CAN TASTE
WHAT YOU ARE EATING.

Day 130

What is the first thing that you do in the morning? Soon, it will be care for your child, but never let your child take the place of God. See if you can still take five minutes before leaving bed to pray and start your day off right.

"My prayer meets you first thing in the morning!"

—PSALM 88:13

Day 129

It is always a good reminder to
us that we need to ask forgiveness
before we can go in front of
a Holy God and talk with him.

"And whenever you stand up to pray,
if you have something against anyone,
forgive so that your Father in heaven
may forgive you your wrongdoings."

—MARK 11:25

Day 128

Do you know what Jesus said
is the most important
commandment of all?

"Our God is the one Lord, and you
must love the Lord your God with all
your heart, with all your being, with all
your mind, and with all your strength."

—MARK 12:29

YOUR BABY IS ABOUT 8
INCHES AND 1 POUND.

Day 127

Women were very important
to Jesus and in his ministry.
You are important as a new mom
but as a woman too!

"When Jesus was in Galilee, these
women had followed and supported
him, along with many other women who
had come to Jerusalem with him."

—MARK 15:41

Day 126—week 23

*I*t is easy for your marriage to suffer when a new child enters your family. The vows you said at your wedding are still important. Make time for just the two of you.

"Love is patient, love is kind, it isn't jealous, it doesn't brag, it isn't arrogant, it isn't rude, it doesn't seek its own advantage, it isn't irritable, it doesn't keep a record of complaints, it isn't happy with injustice, but it is happy with the truth."

—1 Corinthians 13:4-6

Day 125

The love you will have
with this new baby will be
beyond your comprehension.

"Love puts up with all things,
trusts in all things, hopes for all things,
endures all things."

—1 CORINTHIANS 13:7

YOUR BABY CAN SEE THE
DIFFERENCE BETWEEN
LIGHT AND DARK.

Day 124

Nothing requires you to grow up faster than having a child. Suddenly you have a human life completely dependent upon you. Don't be afraid though. God will provide; trust that he will give you wisdom.

"When I was a child, I used to speak like a child, reason like a child, think like a child. But now that I have become a man, I've put an end to childish things."

—1 CORINTHIANS 13:11

Day 123

$\mathcal{D}$uring your pregnancy,
you must be careful
with what you are feeding
your physical body
for your unborn child.
Take as much care
of your spiritual body.

"If there's a physical body, there's
also a spiritual body."

—1 CORINTHIANS 15:44

Day 122

*F*ocus your mind on things
of God. Don't worry
about your baby's future,
but pray for it.

"We don't focus on the things that
can be seen but on the things that can't
be seen. The things that can be seen
don't last, but the things that can't be
seen are eternal."

—2 Corinthians 4:18

Day 121

On the days when life
seems insurmountable,
don't rely on
your own strength;
rely on his.

"So, my child, draw your strength
from the grace that is in Christ Jesus."

—2 TIMOTHY 2:1

Day 120

Can you learn to feel the same
love for fellow believers that you
feel for your child? It may never
be the same, but remember that all
Christians are connected
as part of God's family.

"There are no limits to the affection
that we feel for you."

—2 CORINTHIANS 6:12

YOUR BABY'S FACE
IS FULLY FORMED.

Day 119—week 24

*W*hen God does something wonderful in your life, find someone to share it with. It's so easy to complain, but people appreciate it if you also share your joy with them.

"I will thank you, LORD, with all my heart; I will talk about all your wonderful acts."

—PSALM 9:1

Day 118

*T*he golden rule
is a good rule to follow
and to teach
this unborn child.

"Treat people in the same way that
you want them to treat you."

—LUKE 6:31

Day 117

Take peace in this psalm.
God will be there
for you and
your new baby forever.

"Lord, you have been our help,
generation after generation. Before
the mountains were born, before you
birthed the earth and the inhabited
world—from forever in the past to
forever in the future, you are God."

—PSALM 90:1-2

Day 116

Take each day
and find
the good in it.
Each day is a gift
from God.

"Teach us to number our days
so we can have a wise heart."

—PSALM 90:12

Day 115

Keep your mind
on all the good things
you have in life
instead of dwelling
on the things
you can't change.

"It is good to give thanks to the LORD, to sing praises to your name, Most High."

—PSALM 92:1

Day 114

When you listen to the news and get worried for this new little one you are carrying, take peace that God is in ultimate control.

"Yes, he set the world firmly in place; it won't be shaken."

—Psalm 93:1-2

Your baby is about 9 inches and 1 1/2 pounds.

Day 113

$\mathcal{I}$t is easy to give in
and say yes to your child,
but that is not always
the best thing.

"Train children in the way they
should go; when they grow old, they
won't depart from it."

—Proverbs 22:6

VOCAL CORDS ARE
FUNCTIONING NOW.

Day 112—week 25

$\int$ome women may love seeing their body change as evidence of the child growing; others who have worked to remain in good shape may struggle. Your outside, though, is not what is important. A woman who lives for the Lord is always beautiful.

"Charm is deceptive and beauty fleeting, but a woman who fears the LORD is to be praised."

—PROVERBS 31:30

BEGINNING OF THE
THIRD TRIMESTER

Day 111

*B*e careful of how much you brag about your new baby to others. The Bible is very specific that you should only brag about the Lord.

"*B*ut, the one who brags, should brag in the Lord."

—2 Corinthians 10:17

Day 110

Rest in God that he is giving you the child just right for your family. This child may be different than you expected but is exactly the way God wanted him or her to be.

"I'm afraid that maybe when I come that you will be different from the way I want you to be, and that I'll be different from the way you want me to be."

—2 Corinthians 12:20

Day 109

Remember that it is never
too early to start saving
for this new baby's future.

"It isn't the children's responsibility
to save up for their parents but parents
for children."

—2 CORINTHIANS 12:14

Day 108

Soon you can truly relate to what Paul is trying to say! It is amazing how the words of the Bible hold different meanings at different points in your life. That's why it's said to be "living and active."

"My little children, I'm going through labor pains again until Christ is formed in you."

—GALATIANS 4:19

Day 107

This will be a good verse to remember when you are with a group of women and their babies. Don't compare yourself to them.

"Each person should test their own work and be happy with doing a good job and not compare themselves with others."

—GALATIANS 6:4

Day 106

I am sure you must be
getting tired of being pregnant
by now. Before you know it,
your "harvest"
will be in your arms.

"Let's not get tired of doing good,
because in time we'll have a harvest if we
don't give up."

—GALATIANS 6:9

Day 105—week 26

Can you take one of the fruits
of the spirit and work on one
a week? If you did that,
you would be nine weeks closer
to your baby's birth.

"But the fruit of the Spirit is love,
joy, peace, patience, kindness, goodness,
faithfulness, gentleness, and self-control."

—GALATIANS 5:22-23

Day 104

If you have nights when you cannot sleep, let your mind go over God's promises and all the good things he has done for you.

"I will lie down and fall asleep in peace because you alone, LORD, let me live in safety."

—PSALM 4:8

Day 103

There are so many times we want the easy way out of doing things. Most ladies would probably like to avoid going through labor. Even Jesus did not want to suffer but knew it was what needed to be done.

"He said, 'Father, if it's your will, take this cup of suffering away from me. However, not my will but your will must be done.'"

—LUKE 22:42

Day 102

*J*esus took us all in as family.
Your newborn baby will get
to make the choice if he or she
wants to be a part of his family.

"He replied, 'My mother and
brothers are those who listen to God's
word and do it.'"

—LUKE 8:21

Day 101

God does not want us
to think too highly of ourselves.
Jesus always talks about humility.

"Whoever is least among you all
is the greatest."

—Luke 9:48

Day 100

We think we need all the new
toys and gadgets for our new little
one when what we really need
is to lean on Jesus.

"He has blessed us in Christ with
every spiritual blessing that comes
from heaven."

—EPHESIANS 1:3

YOUR BABY IS NOW
MEASURED FROM HEAD TO
TOE, ABOUT 15 INCHES.

Day 99

Even when we fail, God is always
there to forgive us if we ask.
What a wonderful feeling
as we start on a new adventure
with a new baby!

"God is rich in mercy."

—EPHESIANS 2:4

YOUR BABY HAS MORE TASTE
BUDS RIGHT NOW THAN IT
WILL AT BIRTH.

Day 98—week 27

We are made
to be like God.
Seek his will
for yourself
and your new baby.

"Instead, we are God's
accomplishment, created in
Christ Jesus to do good things."

—EPHESIANS 2:10

Day 97

Right now you are awaiting
the birth of your new baby,
but as you go through the different
stages of being a woman,
seek God's wisdom at every turn.

"Ask and you will receive. Seek and
you will find. Knock and the door will
be opened to you."

—LUKE 11:9-10

Day 96

Is there someone in your birthing class or a friend who needs to learn about Jesus? Pray about who God has put in your path today.

"I tell you, everyone who acknowledges me before humans, the Human One will acknowledge before God's angels."

—LUKE 12:8

Day 95

With all the advertising out there, we want all the newest and best for our new baby. Be careful about being caught in a trap of materialism. Your love will matter much more.

"One's life isn't determined by one's possessions, even when someone is very wealthy."

—LUKE 12:15

Day 94

It's normal to have a great many
concerns about your pregnancy.
Try to give each day to God,
and enjoy the moment.

"Who among you by worrying
can add a single moment to your life?"

—LUKE 12:25

Day 93

Is your heart looking
toward heaven
or toward things
on this earth?

"*W*here your treasure is, there
your heart will be too."

—LUKE 12:34

YOUR BABY IS ABOUT 2 1/2
POUNDS AND 16 INCHES
LONG.

Day 92

*F*ocus today on living
with humility,
gentleness,
and patience.

"Conduct yourselves with all
humility, gentleness, and patience.
Accept each other with love, and make
an effort to preserve the unity of the
Spirit with the peace that ties you
together."

—EPHESIANS 4:2-3

YOUR BABY CAN BLINK.

Day 91—week 28

Are you angry with anyone
today? Don't let a day go by
without attempting to fix this.
Anger and grudges
hurt you more than anyone!

"Be angry without sinning. Don't let
the sun set on your anger."

—EPHESIANS 4:26

Day 90

You can be such a role model to your new baby with how you react to different situations. In order to be able to handle situations the way God wants you to, take time for God and then for yourself.

"Be kind, compassionate, and forgiving to each other, in the same way God forgave you in Christ."

—EPHESIANS 4:32

Day 89

It is easy to say yes to
a child's demands but hard
to say no. If you discipline in love
from an early age, it will be
easier when they are teenagers.

"As for parents, don't provoke
your children to anger, but raise them
with discipline and instruction
about the Lord."

—EPHESIANS 6:4

Day 88

How is your new baby going
to learn to obey you? You need
to be consistent, loving, and patient
as he or she explores a new world.

"Children, obey your parents
in everything, because this pleases
the Lord."

—COLOSSIANS 3:20

Day 87

You need to remember
as your baby grows that he
or she is his or her own individual
person and will not always think
and act like you would want him or
her to. Encourage your children
to be individuals who honor
God through their unique talents.

"Parents, don't provoke your
children in a way that ends up
discouraging them."

—COLOSSIANS 3:21

Day 86

*R*emember that
you only have
to please God,
not everyone else
in your life.

"Whatever you do, do it from the
heart for the Lord and not for people."

—COLOSSIANS 3:23

YOUR BABY IS ABOUT
17 INCHES AND 3 POUNDS.

Day 85

You can ask God anything,
but don't forget to thank him
for all he has already done for you.

"Keep on praying and guard your
prayers with thanksgiving."

—COLOSSIANS 4:2

Day 84—week 29

Just as you will be kind
and loving to your new baby,
make sure you are also kind and
loving to those around you, whether
they return the favor or not.

"Instead, we were gentle with
you like a nursing mother caring
for her own children."

—1 THESSALONIANS 2:7

Day 83

$\mathcal{I}$t is healthy for children to do things on their own without you. Even though this will be hard at first, you will always carry them in your heart, as they will with you.

"Brothers and sisters, we were separated from you for a while physically but not in our hearts."

—1 Thessalonians 2:17

Day 82

God wants us to be peaceful
and joyful. Turn on that radio
and sing to him! He hears you
in perfect pitch.

"Sing to the LORD a new song!
Sing to the LORD, all the earth!"

—PSALM 96:1

Day 81

The Bible was written down
so all people will remember God's
word. It might be fun for you
to write in a journal during your
pregnancy and through the years of
your child's life. Share it when your
child is an adult—perhaps when he
or she is preparing for parenthood!

"Let this be written down for the
next generation so that people not yet
created will praise the LORD."

—PSALM 102:18

Day 80

We can be so hard on ourselves as women and mothers. Realize God is our only judge, and he loves us.

"The LORD is compassionate and merciful, very patient, and full of faithful love."

—PSALM 103:8

Day 79

Let's get this out there right now: you will never be a perfect mom. That's okay! If we have given our life over to God, he will love us through all our mistakes, as will your children.

"He doesn't deal with us according to our sin or repay us according to our wrongdoing, because as high as heaven is above the earth, that's how large God's faithful love is for those who honor him."

—PSALM 103:10-11

Day 78

*I*f you are blessed to still have your mom around or your husband's mom, ask her questions about your pregnancy or raising your baby. Don't be prideful—she has a wealth of information you have yet to learn. Nobody knows everything.

"There's nothing new under the sun. People may say about something: 'Look at this! It's new!' But it was already around for ages before us."

—ECCLESIASTES 1:9-10

Day 77—week 30

Whether in the Old Testament,
the New Testament, or even today,
God will always be
your strength and shield.

"God is indeed my salvation; I will
trust and won't be afraid. Yah, the LORD,
is my strength and my shield; he has
become my salvation."

—ISAIAH 12:2

YOUR BABY CAN REGULATE
BODY TEMPERATURE.

Day 76

God wants us to have joy in our lives. Find something to smile about each day. Even on the hardest day, God will provide something to bring happiness (blooming flowers, the smell of spring rain, the call of a friend). It is simply our job to look for those moments.

"So all Israel brought up the chest containing the LORD's convenant with shouts of joy, accompanied by the blast of the ram's horn, by trumpets and cymbals, and playing on harps and lyres."

—1 CHRONICLES 15:28

Day 75

A simple verse
but one of the
hardest
to live out.

"Rejoice always. Pray continually.
Give thanks in every situation because
this is God's will for you in Christ Jesus."

—1 Thessalonians 5:16-18

Day 74

It is never too early to start praying for your children's futures. Pray that God would make them men and women who honor him.

"We are constantly praying for you for this: that our God will make you worthy of his calling and accomplish every good desire and faithful work by his power."

—2 THESSALONIANS 1:11

Day 73

You cannot discipline
or instruct your baby yet,
but you can prepare yourself
by having a pure heart,
a good conscience,
and a sincere faith.

"The goal of instruction is love
from a pure heart, a good conscience,
and a sincere faith."

—1 TIMOTHY 1:5

Day 72

It is important to pray for our leaders, who will make decisions that will affect your child's future.

"Pray for kings and everyone who is in authority so that we can live a quiet and peaceful life in complete godliness and dignity."

—1 TIMOTHY 2:2

YOUR BABY IS ABOUT 18 INCHES LONG AND OVER 3 POUNDS.

Day 71

$\mathscr{R}$espect for other people is an
integral part of Christianity.
It is important that you live this
out for your children to see.

"Treat older women like your
mother, and treat younger women like
your sisters with appropriate respect."

—1 TIMOTHY 5:2

YOUR BABY'S BRAIN CAN
PROCESS INFORMATION, TRACK
LIGHT, AND PERCEIVE SOUND.

Day 70—week 31

Remember this verse when you are in the grocery store with your little one or at church. It is important to be consistent with your little one, even when it is hard.

"Be ready to do it whether it is convenient or inconvenient. Correct, confront, and encourage with patience and instruction."

—2 TIMOTHY 4:2

Day 69

*W*hen you are with other people,
be careful what you say and hear.
This is especially true
when little ears are near.

"*A*void their godless discussions,
because they will lead many people into
ungodly behavior, and their ideas will
spread like an infection."

—2 TIMOTHY 2:16-17

Day 68

Before this new baby comes, take time to read God's word. Your day is very busy and will only get busier, but life will be more peaceful if you find time for God.

"Every scripture is inspired by God and is useful for teaching, for showing mistakes, for correcting, and for training character, so that the person who belongs to God can be equipped to do everything that is good."

—2 TIMOTHY 3:16-17

Day 67

Patience is a key virtue with kids!
Just as you will learn to be patient
with them, also be patient
with God as you wait on him
at different points in your life.

"Abraham obtained the promise
by showing patience."

—HEBREWS 6:15

Day 66

When you read about God's
promises to you and future
generations, rest in his promises
because you have a God
who is trustworthy.

"It's impossible for God to lie."

—Hebrews 6:18

Your baby has moved
into birthing position.

Day 65

*I*s there anyone you can reach out
to and show God's love to today?
You just might inspire him or her
to do it for someone else.

"Let's also think about how to
motivate each other to show love
and to do good works."

—HEBREWS 10:24

YOUR BABY IS ABOUT
4 POUNDS AND 19 INCHES.

Day 64

$\mathcal{A}$t this point, you cannot see your baby, but you know he or she is there. In the same way, just because you cannot see God does not mean that he's not there.

"$\mathcal{F}$aith is the reality of what we hope for, the proof of what we don't see."

—HEBREWS 11:1

Day 63—week 32

You are in a "race"
from day 280
to the birth
of your baby.
Run that race well.

"So then let's also run the race
that is laid out in front of us."

—HEBREWS 12:1

YOUR BABY'S SKIN IS NO
LONGER SEE-THROUGH.

Day 62

As you raise this child, you may find yourself saying and doing things that your parents did when you were little! If you find that you still use your parents' advice today, take time to call them and thank them for all they did for you.

"Listen, my son, to your father's instruction; don't neglect your mother's teaching."

—PROVERBS 1:8

Day 61

This is such an important verse, especially as you help your new baby learn and grow.

"Everyone should be quick to listen, slow to speak, and slow to grow angry."

—JAMES 1:19

Day 60

As you get closer to your due date, there are going to be days as your body changes that you are being tested in the physical sense. Hang in there, and know God is with you at every step.

"Those who stand firm during testing are blessed. They are tried and true. They will receive the life God has promised to those who love him as their reward."

—JAMES 1:12

Day 59

Ask God for his wisdom,
and he will give it to you.

"Teach me to do what pleases you,
because you are my God."

—Psalm 143:10

Day 58

*M*oney is not evil in itself.
It can do a lot of good, but if you
are not satisfied with what you
have, you will teach this dangerous
mentality to your new baby.

"The love of money is the root of all
kinds of evil."

—1 TIMOTHY 6:10

YOUR BABY IS ABOUT
4 1/2 POUNDS.

Day 57

*Y*ou will have new experiences
during your pregnancy whether it
is your first time or your fourth.
Wake up in the morning asking God
to be with you to overcome any
new challenges you may face.

"Be our strength every morning, our
salvation in times of distress."

—Isaiah 33:2

Antibodies are being passed
from you to your baby.

Day 56—week 33

*A*lways be on the look-out for new experiences you can show your new baby as he or she grows up. You will be amazed at what you will learn along the way.

"Don't withhold instruction from children."

—PROVERBS 23:13

Day 55

Teach your child to be good soil.
It is your job as a parent to help
raise children who are receptive
to the word of God, but
it will be their job in the end
to make the decision to follow God.

"The seed scattered on good soil
are those who hear the word and
embrace it."

—MARK 4:20

Day 54

Children are so innocent.
They will trust what you teach them
about Jesus at an early age.
It is important for you to lay
the correct foundation.
But just as they will learn from you,
you will learn from them.

"Those who humble themselves like
this little child will be the greatest in the
kingdom of heaven."

—MATTHEW 18:4

Day 53

Look out your window right now
and marvel at God's handiwork.
When you feel your baby kick,
think of God and how amazing he is.
He is the one who is making
this new child inside of you.

"You established both the moon
and the sun. You set all the boundaries
of the earth in place. Summer and
winter? You made them!"

—PSALM 74:16-17

Day 52

Don't fret about your delivery.
Take one day at a time
and leave the rest to God.

"Therefore, stop worrying about
tomorrow, because tomorrow will worry
about itself."

—MATTHEW 6:34

Day 51

You may not feel at your most beautiful at this point in your pregnancy, but you are. Even more important is what is inside of you.

"Like a gold ring in a pig's nose is a beautiful woman who lacks discretion."

—PROVERBS 11:22

YOUR BABY IS ABOUT
5 POUNDS AND 20 INCHES.

Day 50

If you are awake in the middle
of the night because your body is
uncomfortable with the little guest
inside, keep your mind busy
by counting your blessings!

"My mouth speaks praise with joy
on my lips—whenever I ponder you on
my bed, whenever I meditate on you in
the middle of the night."

—PSALM 63:5-6

Day 49—week 34

A mature rating on a movie
or a video game implies violence,
swearing, and inappropriate conduct,
but is all of that really mature?
Help your children grow up
in the ways of God, not
in the ways of today's society.

"Brothers and sisters, don't be like
children in the way you think. Well,
be babies when it comes to evil, but be
adults in your thinking."

—1 CORINTHIANS 14:20

Day 48

Even if you are having trouble
getting out of and into your bed
because of the baby,
wake up and praise God.
Have your last thoughts be of him.
Make it a habit to wake up each
morning with God's blessings in mind.

"Proclaim your loyal love in the
morning, your faithfulness at nighttime."

—Psalm 92:2

Day 47

We have all seen children who are out of control in stores. While sometimes this can be the result of bad parenting, sometimes it is simply the result of a very long, tiring day! Nevertheless, love your child enough to teach him or her to respect you and others. You have a blank slate to work on with this new baby.

"The rod and correction lead to wisdom, but children out of control shame their mothers."

—PROVERBS 29:15

Day 46

Being a mom brings
such an understanding
of God's love for us.
Having a child
will bring you
even closer to God.

"Like a person feels compassion
for their children—that's how the LORD
feels compassion for those who
honor him."

—PSALM 103:13

Day 45

The Lord is present
in every good thing.
All you need to do
is look for him.

"May he encourage your hearts
and give you strength in every good
thing you do or say."

—2 THESSALONIANS 2:17

Day 44

Take time today
to pray for you, your family,
and your new baby. Don't
forget to take a moment
and really think about
all God has done for you.

"Come near to God, and he will
come near to you."

—JAMES 4:8

TERM PREGNANCY
BEGINS TODAY.

Day 43

*O*nce you become part
of God's family, you will live
forever. That is why it is so
important to help your new baby
learn about God and his love.

"You have a pure and enduring
inheritance that cannot perish—an
inheritance that is presently kept safe in
heaven for you."

—1 PETER 1:4

YOUR BABY IS ABOUT
20 INCHES LONG
AND 5 1/2 POUNDS.

Day 42—week 35

How pleased God is when we
praise him in our everyday life,
even when it is the
same old thing!

"Your genuine faith will result in
praise, glory, and honor for you when
Jesus Christ is revealed. Although you've
never seen him, you love him."

—1 PETER 1:7-8

BRAIN DEVELOPS
AT A RAPID RATE NOW.

Day 41

It is easy to love God when things are going well. It is much harder when you are tired, your feet hurt, and you just want to give birth! Praise him anyway.

"If any of you are suffering, they should pray. If any of you are happy, they should sing."

—James 5:13

Day 40

*Y*our baby is so pure when he or she is born. What a great example to learn from.

"Therefore, get rid of all ill will and all deceit, pretense, envy, and slander. Instead, like a newborn baby, desire the pure milk of the word. Nourished by it, you will grow into salvation, since you have tasted that the Lord is good."

—1 Peter 2:1-3

Your baby should be settled in a head-down position.

Day 39

We have a
God-sized hole in us
that can only
be filled with God.

"The people whose God is the LORD
are truly happy!"

—PSALM 144:15

Day 38

You will learn so much from this new child of yours. He or she will teach you to slow down and enjoy the moment. Watch how long it takes to eat one Cheerio and how long it takes you to eat a whole bowl. Let your new child remind you to slow down and enjoy life.

"I assure you that whoever doesn't welcome God's kingdom like a child will never enter it."

—LUKE 18:17

Day 37

*Y*ou may be waiting
for God to answer
a certain prayer.
Don't give up.
His time is not our time.

"Don't let it escape your notice, dear
friends, that with the Lord a single day
is like a thousand years and a thousand
years are like a single day."

—2 PETER 3:8

 YOUR BABY IS ABOUT
6 POUNDS AND 20 INCHES.

Day 36

*W*e each need to look at ourselves
in a mirror and admit to God where we
have made mistakes, and he will forgive
us, though there still could be some
consequences to what we did.
You will see this with your new baby.
Your love will forgive,
but your child must still learn.

"*I*f we claim, 'We don't have any sin,'
we deceive ourselves and the truth is
not in us. But if we confess our sins, he
is faithful and just to forgive us our sins
and cleanse us from everything we've
done wrong."

—1 JOHN 1:8-9

Day 35—week 36

As parents, we need to teach our children to live out what they believe. Words are easy, but one must follow up with actions.

"Little children, let's not love with words or speech but with action and truth."

—1 John 3:18

Day 34

We like to think that God should give us whatever we ask for. The Bible is very clear, though, that God will only say yes to prayers that are within his will. He wants what's best for you and won't let you settle for anything else.

"If we ask for anything in agreement with his will, he listens to us."

—1 JOHN 5:14

Day 33

Sometimes I think we make God
too small. Look up at the sky and
then down at your belly
and consider the God who can
create such a big sky and then
such a small, precious bundle.

"Look up at the sky and consider:
Who created these?"

—Isaiah 40:26

Day 32

From the minute you wake up and get out of bed until you rest your head on the pillow at night, try to think of the good things the Lord has done for you. Even your changing body means you have new life in you.

"From sunrise to sunset, let the LORD's name be praised!"

—PSALM 113:3

Day 31

*T*ake comfort in the fact
that a merciful and holy God
loves you and your new baby.

"The Lᴏʀᴅ is merciful and
righteous; our God is compassionate."

—Psᴀʟᴍ 116:5

Day 30

*J*ust as your love will never die
for this new baby, God's love
will never cease for you both.

"Give thanks to the LORD because
he is good, because his faithful love
lasts forever."

—PSALM 118:1

IF YOUR BABY WAS BORN
TODAY, IT WOULD BE
CONSIDERED FULL TERM.

Day 29

*R*est in the fact that
God will love your baby
all through his or her life
and then his or her
children and so on.

"Your faithfulness extends from
one generation to the next!"

—PSALM 119:90

Day 28—week 37

God is a mighty God. Remember today that although he is a friend, he is also the King of Kings.

"You wear light like a robe; you open the skies like a curtain. You build your lofty house on the waters; you make the clouds your chariot."

—Psalm 104:2-3

Day 27

Look at yourself in the mirror
and realize that God made you
and loves you. He made you wisely
even though at times you
may not feel it—believe it!

"Lord, you have done so many
things! You made them all so wisely!
The earth is full of your creations!"

—Psalm 104:24

Day 26

What a gift to be able to bring a new life into this world. When you feel your baby kick inside your womb, you may wonder how people can doubt God. Is this child merely an accident of fate? Surely not! Seek after the God who made you with all your heart.

"Just fear the LORD and serve him faithfully with all your heart. Look at what great things he has done for you!"

—1 SAMUEL 12:24

Day 25

Love this new child, care for
it, make it a priority, but do not
worship it. God still must come first.
No one will deny that
this is incredibly hard, but it is
also incredibly important.

"I strengthen you—though you don't
know me—so all will know, from the
rising of the sun to its setting, that there
is nothing apart from me."

—Isaiah 45:5-6

Day 24

God already knows everything about your child—what you will name him or her, what he or she will be like in school, who he or she will marry, and so on.

"The LORD called me before my birth, called my name when I was in my mother's womb."

—ISAIAH 49:1

YOUR BABY IS ABOUT
7 POUNDS AND 20 INCHES.

Day 23

The Bible is a living book that will teach you things at each stage of your life. When you are a new mom, a mom of teens, or a grandmother, it will continue to teach you new things.

"The first thing to know about your word is that it is true and that all your righteous rules last forever."

—PSALM 119:160

Day 22

This world can be tough. You might listen to the news and wonder what you're bringing your new baby into. Keep your eyes up, focused on God, and he will bring you peace. Even when it doesn't look like it, God is still in control.

"I raise my eyes toward the mountains. Where will my help come from? My help comes from the LORD, the maker of heaven and earth."

—PSALM 121:1-2

Day 21—week 38

Isn't it wonderful to know our God is compassionate and cares about everything you are doing?

"My heart winces within me; my compassion grows warm and tender."

—HOSEA 11:8

Day 20

All your family and extended family are excited to meet this new baby. It can be wonderful to be a part of an extended family. You may never love your in-laws in the same way you love your own parents, but make an effort to reach out to them. They are now an important part of your life as well as your new child's.

"Look at how good and pleasing it is when families live together as one!"

—Psalm 133:1

Day 19

A god is not simply a golden calf.
Material goods, family members,
and goals can all become gods.
Keep the Lord first.

"I am the first, and I am the last, and
besides me there are no gods."

—ISAIAH 44:6

Day 18

It is harder for you to get around now. This is a time to ask God to give you the strength you need to get through these next few weeks.

"Those who hope in the LORD will renew their strength; they will fly up on wings like eagles; they will run and not be tired; they will walk and not be weary."

—ISAIAH 40:31

Day 17

As you are drawing nearer
to your due date, give God
all your anxious thoughts.
He can handle them.

"Throw all your anxiety onto him,
because he cares about you."

—1 PETER 5:7

Day 16

You get to meet your new gift
from the Lord very soon.

"No doubt about it: children are
a gift from the LORD; the fruit of the
womb is a divine reward."

—PSALM 127:3

Day 15

You will not make your baby come
any earlier by worrying.
Enjoy today and every day
before your baby comes.

"Therefore, stop worrying about
tomorrow, because tomorrow will
worry about itself."

—MATTHEW 6:34

Day 14—week 39

*N*ow that your baby is almost here, you will start the job of parenting that you have spent the last nine months preparing for.

"*S*tay awake, stand firm in your faith, be brave, be strong. Everything should be done in love."

—1 CORINTHIANS 16:13

Day 13

This baby that you will soon meet
was made just for your family.
This does not mean that your child
will be just like you or anyone else
in your family. Learn and grow
from your child's differences.
Each person is unique.

"But God had set me apart from
birth and called me through his grace."

—GALATIANS 1:15

Day 12

$\mathcal{D}$uring labor,
God will be with you.

"He listened when I cried out
to him for help."

—Psalm 22:24

Day 11

*I*n the delivery room, take hold
of God's hand as you bring forth
this new life. Take time now
to memorize a few verses to cling
to as you give birth.

"Trust in God; I won't be afraid.
What can mere flesh do to me?"

—Psalm 56:4

Day 10

You will soon be a new mom with a precious baby to love. If you are ever at a loss as to what to pray, have peace that the Holy Spirit is praying for you.

"The Spirit comes to help our weakness. We don't know what we should pray, but the Spirit himself pleads our case with unexpressed groans."

—ROMANS 8:26

Day 9

Mary was blessed to carry
the Son of God. You are blessed
to carry this new child. Just as God
had a purpose for his son, he
also has a purpose for your child.

"With a loud voice she [Elizabeth]
blurted out, 'God has blessed you above
all women, and he has blessed the child
you carry.'"

—LUKE 1:42

Day 8

After Jesus was born, Mary
remembered the wonderful things
that happened. Even as the years go
by, you will remember the first time
you met your child with amazement.
What a gift God gives us
each day of our child's life.

"Mary committed these things to
memory and considered them carefully."

—LUKE 2:19

Day 7—week 40

When you gaze at your new baby in your arms, you will realize that you would do anything for this precious bundle that is so dependent on you. God, who has perfect love, loves you even more.

"If you who are evil know how to give good gifts to your children, how much more will the heavenly Father give the Holy Spirit to those who ask him?"

—LUKE 11:13

Day 6

*W*e cannot put God into a box
of our making. He is beyond
what we can even imagine. He loves
you and this new baby
more than you can fathom.

"For I am God and not a human
being, the holy one in your midst."

—HOSEA 11:9

Day 5

As you're facing childbirth,
remember that though the pain
is intense, it is fleeting compared
to the joy of first meeting
your son or daughter.

"When a woman gives birth, she has
pain because her time has come.
But when the child is born, she no
longer remembers her distress because
of her joy that a child has been born
into the world."

—JOHN 16:21

Day 4

$\mathcal{T}$ake comfort in this verse as you are approaching the birth of your child. God is with you at all times.

"Whenever anything happens,
I am there."

—Isaiah 48:16

Day 3

This is the last line
in the Bible.
As you come to the end
of your pregnancy,
may you feel
his grace with you.

"The grace of the Lord Jesus
be with all."

—REVELATION 22:21

Day 2

It's been our honor to be a part of your pregnancy despite not knowing you. Give your precious baby a kiss for us. Congratulations!

"You in turn should greet each other with a holy kiss."

—1 Corinthians 16:20

Day 1

This is our prayer for you.
May God be with you
and your new family.

"May the Lord of peace himself give
you peace always in every way. The Lord
be with all of you."

—2 THESSALONIANS 3:16